*This book is for:*

_____

*From:*

_____

*Date:*

_____

# FROM Bread AND Wine TO Saints Divine

## Anthony DeStefano

### Illustrated by James Madsen

SOPHIA INSTITUTE PRESS
Manchester, NH

This book is dedicated to my brother,
Fr. Salvatore DeStefano
of the Archdiocese of New York.

– *Anthony DeStefano*

# SOPHIA
## INSTITUTE PRESS

Text Copyright © 2024 by Anthony DeStefano
Images Copyright © 2024 by James Madsen

Bible quotations are from the RSVCE.

Printed in the United States of America.

Sophia Institute Press®
Box 5284, Manchester, NH 03108
1-800-888-9344

www.SophiaInstitute.com

Sophia Institute Press® is a registered
trademark of Sophia Institute.

Print ISBN: 979-8-88911-384-3

Library of Congress Control Number: 2024952369

First Printing, 2025

# From the Bible

As they were eating, Jesus took bread, and blessed, and broke it, and gave it to the disciples and said, "*Take, eat; this is my body.*" And he took a cup, and when he had given thanks he gave it to them, saying, "*Drink of it, all of you; for this is my blood of the covenant, which is poured out for many for the forgiveness of sins.*"

— *Matthew 26:26–28*

Jesus said to them, "*I am the bread of life; he who comes to me shall not hunger, and he who believes in me shall never thirst.*"

— *John 6:35*

"*I am the living bread which came down from heaven; if anyone eats of this bread, he will live forever; and the bread which I shall give for the life of the world is my flesh… Truly, truly, I say to you, unless you eat the flesh of the Son of man and drink his blood, you have no life in you; he who eats my flesh and drinks my blood has eternal life, and I will raise him up at the last day. For my flesh is food indeed, and my blood is drink indeed. He who eats my flesh and drinks my blood abides in me, and I in him. As the living Father sent me, and I live because of the Father, so he who eats me will live because of me. This is the bread which came down from heaven, not such as the fathers ate and died; he who eats this bread will live forever.*"

— *John 6:51–58*

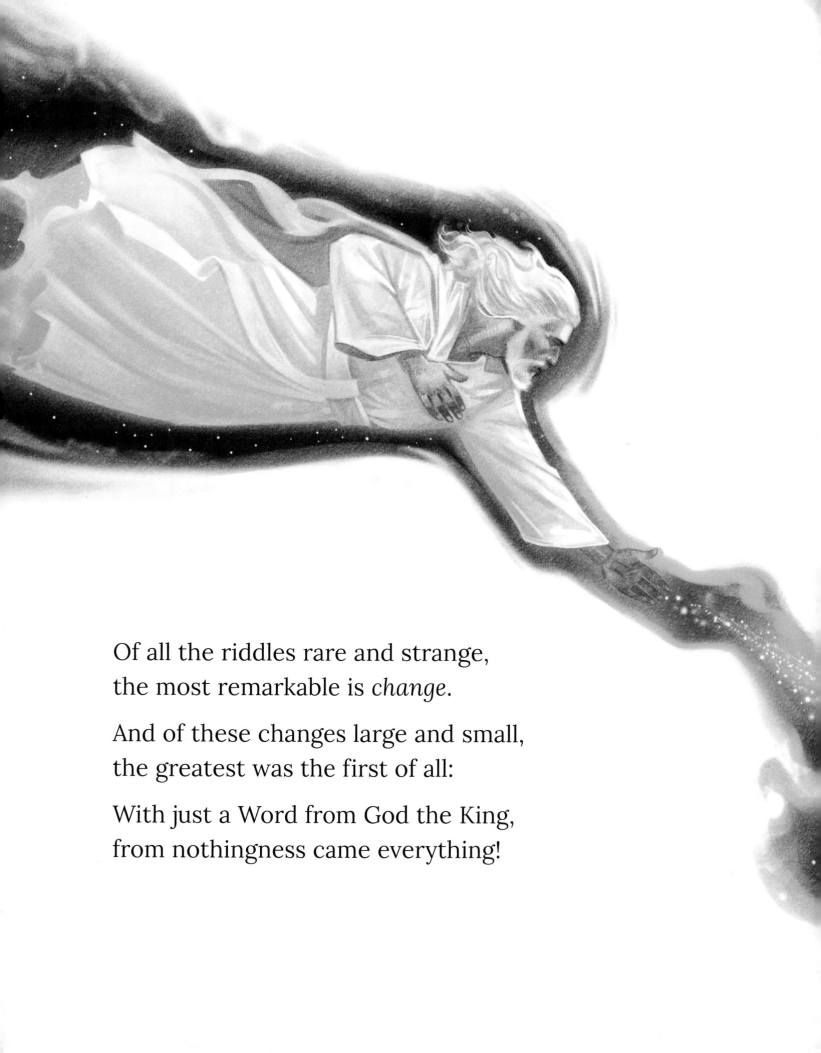

Of all the riddles rare and strange,
the most remarkable is *change*.

And of these changes large and small,
the greatest was the first of all:

With just a Word from God the King,
from nothingness came everything!

Why did God create all this?
To share His love and happiness.

How He caused this great change, though, is something that we just don't know.

And so it's been through history. Change remains a mystery.

Seasons change
from green to gold,

with warming sun
and chilling cold.

A dark and scary stormy night
transforms by morning into light.

An unborn baby, fresh and new,
becomes a boy or girl like you.

A caterpillar waves goodbye
and soon becomes a butterfly.

Sprinkle seeds with springtime showers;
time goes by, and you'll have flowers.

Store some eggs and incubate...

and chicks will hatch there while you wait.

Plant an acorn in the ground;
soon an oak tree will be found.

Leave water in the freezer now;
cubes of ice will form somehow.

Stir sugar, flour, eggs, then bake.

Presto! There's a birthday cake!

A box of crayons at the start…

becomes the most amazing art.

Logs of wood that burn in fire
reduce to ash when flames expire.

Lumps of coal deep in the earth
compress to diamonds of great worth.

Life is full of transformations
surpassing all our expectations.

But awesome as these changes are,
one outshines them all by far:

A mix of wheat and water, spread,
flattens out and turns to bread.

A grape that's hand-picked from a vine
ages and becomes a wine.

This special bread and wine are made,

and to the church they're both conveyed.

A priest at Mass then lifts them up:
at first the bread, and then the cup.

He says some words that might sound odd,
and bread and wine turn into...GOD!

Yes, Jesus Christ, who saved us all
has now become so very small.

He has the power to exist—
present in the *Eucharist*.

But why is He so small and slim?
*So we can change and be like Him!*

So boys and girls like me and you
can walk up humbly, two by two,

Faithful children, in a line,
there to eat the bread divine.

Then as months and years go past,
deep inside, WE change at last!

Receiving God in faith this way,
we grow more holy every day.

We learn to share and sacrifice
no matter what the loss or price.

We grow in courage, truth, and love,
just like the saints of God, above.

Of all the changes here and there,
of all the changes everywhere,
of all the changes near and far,
of all the changes that there are,
of all the changes bright and blessed…

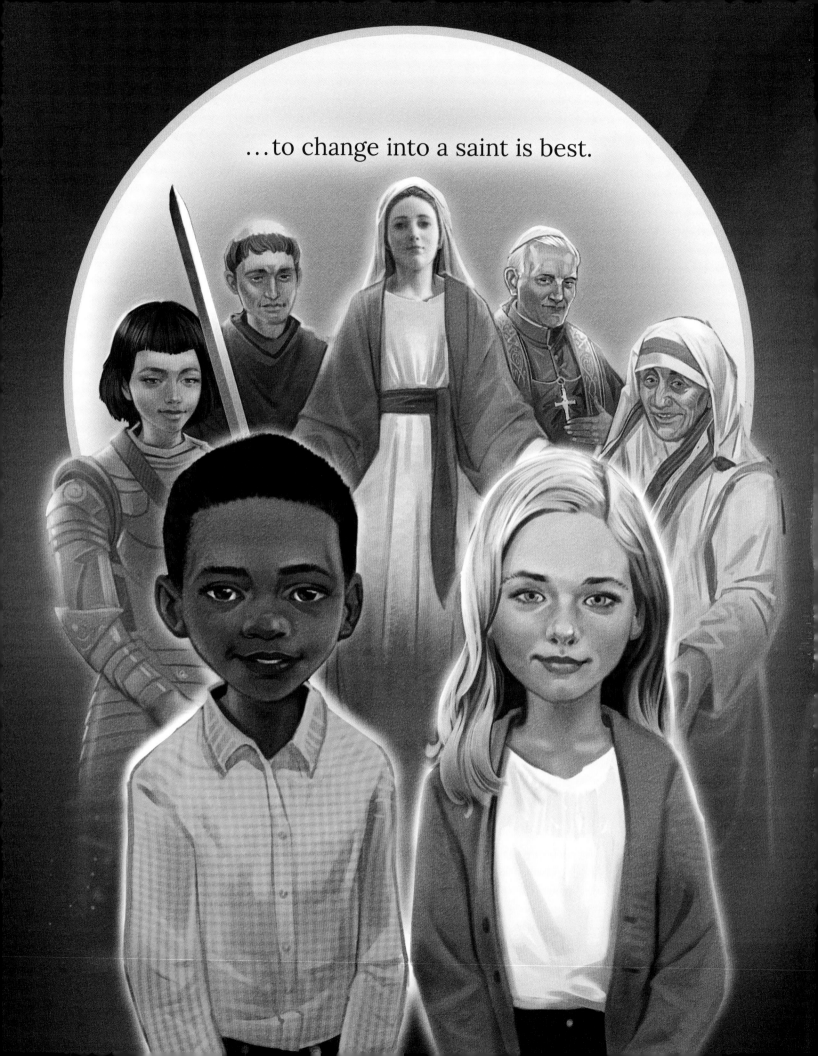

...to change into a saint is best.